£2-00

15/11

It's like walking a tightrope

Mary Farrell

It's like walking a tightrope – Mary Farrell

impspired@gmail.com

ISBN: 978-1-914130-24-3

It's like walking a tightrope – Mary Farrell

OTHER TITLES BY IMPSPIRED

Earth Magicke –
by Margaret Royall

Periodic Stories -
By Jim Bates

Stepping Up –
By DC Diamondopolous

The Blue, Red Lyrae
By Mehreen Ahmed

Shiloh Osheen –
By As Viewed by a Poet Protagonist

Lost in Thought –
By Charlie M. Zamarripa

Habits of Totem –
By Ivan Peledov

A review by Jim Simpson, Author of *Smokes and Birds*, (Dingle Publishing 2021)

What a telling title. Mary Farrell brings her considerable skills to bear as she juxtaposes the idyllic with the brutal, the dream with the visceral. Her keen observation of flora and fauna shines through time and again, in a sensitive appreciation of colour and love of natural beauty. But she also confronts the cruelty of life; the finality of death. The stark reality of disappointment and isolation. Her style is imaginative and inventive. She has a particular facility with ekphrasis, taking a work of art and making it her own. She grasps the opportunity to use the compound word, to exploit alliteration, to invent metaphor with great effect. Her considerable achievement is not prescribed by form as she turns her hand easily from prose to poetry. This is a varied and adventurous collection, which employs great richness of language, invokes the magical, but never dodges the difficult.

For Jamie

Contents

Introduction

Mary Farrell joined her first Creative Writing class in 2017 on returning from France to live in Northern Ireland. Now a Facilitator of the North Coast Writing Group, she is also a member of the Judging Panel for the weekly Reedsy Prompts Competitions and was an Auditor for the First- and Third-Year Creative Writing Courses at UU University in Northern Ireland in 2019/2020. With both Poetry and Prose published in a variety of magazines and anthologies, she has read her own work at Open Mic Sessions, on the Tenx9 stage and on BBC Radio Ulster. Having completed a Trilogy of sixty short stories – the prologues of which are at the end of this Collection - she has now begun another series of twenty short stories called 'The Street'.

'It's like Walking a Tightrope' is her first Collection and contains a selection from the many pieces she has written over the last four years. Some pieces grew without restraint, others were trained to flourish within restricted word counts-less than 1000, less than 100 and in one case less than 50. Some were written to be read on the printed page, others were to be heard as performance pieces. A few were written especially for literary competitions. They have all have been nurtured over time, nourished by the support of others, and then were finally pruned by the fiercest of literary topiary. Many other seedlings sadly never reached the light of day and still languish in the depths of her laptop. It has indeed been a 'tightrope walk' to find the right phrases and leave out others, to balance wordcounts and to move forward with consistency. She will continue to practice however, hoping to improve her acrobatic skills.

Acknowledgements

Anyone involved in the Creative Writing world knows that it is a very generous and supportive one, but there are a few people in particular whom I would like to thank.

The members of the North Coast Writers Group have been unflagging in their friendship, support and creative advice. It is a pleasure indeed to work with such a team.

I have also been made a very welcome member of the Portrush Writers Group, led by Kate Murphy, and This Writing Thing, a North-West writing Group led by Sue Divin. Many thanks to these two ladies also – along with Jim Simpson, and Kathleen McCracken of UU University – for their time and expertise when they read the Collection before it was published and made such kind comments.

I am very grateful indeed to Maureen Hamilton for the time she spent, and her attention to detail, when she was editing these pieces. Her tightening and polishing skills are deeply appreciated, as is her friendship.

Without Steve Cawte, the Editor of Impspired Press, this Collection would literally not exist. His support, advice and editing expertise – quite apart from his continual good humour and seemingly endless patience - made the whole 'birthing' process a much easier experience than I could ever have dreamt.

Finally, I would like to thank Alexander, Taylor and Charlie for the love, hugs, smiles and laughter they brought into my life during the years when these pieces were written.

Acknowledgements:-

A Matter of Time - Read by the writer on BBC Radio Ulster, 'Time of our Lives' programme, September 30th, 2018, *An autobiographical Tale*- Performed on the Stage at an Tenx9 event , October 2019, *Plenty of Fish* - Read at an Open Mic Session at Harrys Shack, Portstewart, Autumn, 2019, *A Tale of a Barn* - Winner of the Lurig Drama Club Competition, 2020, Read by the actor Ciaran Hinds, November 26th, 2020 @ www.thenineglens.com, *At the Fork*- First published Flash Fiction Magazine, April 2020, *The Clash* -First Published by Sledgehammer Magazine, June, 2021, *Beware of Woodpeckers, The Cold light of day, Backfire, The Cracking of the Mirror* -First Published by Impspired Anthology #5, September, 2021, *Winter Solstice* -First published in the 2019 CAP Anthology, 'Find'.

It's like walking a tightrope – Mary Farrell

The Clash

Gulls dive-bomb the promenade debris. The high tide tries to suck the harbour walls out to sea. A windblown chip paper clamps her leg as she walks, head down. A question turns in her like an old-fashioned mangle. *Should I stay or should I go?*

If she stays, he'll eventually find her and take revenge for her leaving….on her body, on her psyche. No scars on one , a trench-deep cicatrix on the other. If she moves on, then where to? Would that become her life-pattern? He'd soon work out there were only a handful of seaside towns with happy memories for her. He'd find her. But the same spark in her which had driven her to flight, now reacts against being continual prey. She decides. It has to end here.

The wind splays her hair which weaves a nimbus round her head. She is Medusa. One hand in her pocket, she slots her fingers into the grip of the gun. The other hand she places on her swollen belly, a gesture of affection and defiance. Showdown time.

Magpie Blues on the Coming of May

My window frames
bucolic peace
but is haunted
of late by a
swooping swirling
seeking searching
solitary soulmate.
A single magpie
-sorrow indeed-
wraiths through trees and fields
open-winged open-hearted
questing a nesting mate
in usual Spring cycle
alone its imprint
etches dark
on compassionate eyes

But wait…
Today's dawn chorused
two voices not one.
What Beltane ballet
did you perform
in last night's gloaming
to seduce another
singleton

and now bring joy instead?

Beware of Woodpeckers

"You've forgotten me" Mrs Faraday accused him on his arrival at the Pasadena Lorenzo Inn. She was right! His last time there, so much had been happening he had little recollection of the Motel manageress.

Now here she was in front of him, with her sharp little beak poking into his psyche to unlock doors firmly shut for eleven months. Quivering with unsated curiosity, her eyes were pecking, prising their way into his brain, his soul. How she thirsted to know every nuance, every detail…but there was really only one overriding fact.

Eloise Cortes was dead.

She had plunged from a third-floor balcony to lie spread-eagled poolside. A stain beneath her spread wine-dark on the shadowed tiles.

He could hear Mrs Faraday thinking, "Did she fall or was she pushed?"

He deleted her thought, an instinct for self-preservation wiping his mental blackboard clean. As the returning Investigative Detective on a newly re-opened case, he had to be unemotional, have clear perspective. But even eleven months later his mind still totally recoiled from the scene, from the memory of her arm sliding out of his grasp as she flew.

He had loved Eloise so much!

Books and covers

A handsome muscular Colombian barista, used to admiring eyes, serves a brown wren of a middle-aged matron in a moth-eaten tweed coat. He has already decided he is not going to waste his charm. The cheap china saucer slams onto the table, the overflow of coffee brown-soaking the two sachets of sugar. A silvered spoon clatters onto the beige lino tablecloth with a dull thud. Outwardly she meekly accepts his lack of courtesy. Inwardly she smiles, her nose wrinkling with anticipated pleasure. Her review in tomorrow's paper will flatten his arrogance, stop his strutting.

Winter Window

Silent-whimpering, withering
rime fingers smudged by a milky sun
lone leaves cling cub-like to the maternal
underbelly of bare branches
bough bark slither-slimed with icy
droplets scattered by a hesitant dawn

over the hill-rim
light crawls grip-grab
up a lifeless slate sky
dawning reflective ley-lines
on dewdrops strung-stretched
on sentinel stiff grass

Earth heartbeats muted
somnolence spreads numbing freeze
unwilling just yet to shake
its blanket cover of quilted dark
tucked in by horizonal hands
I duck back down under winters cover

Splitting Seconds

In the River Severn there is a bore, and flowing into the Severn is another river, the Usk, cutting through the Welsh hills past the mines, past the sheep-filled fields, past the age-old settlement of Caerleon. Like most courses going from hill to sea, the water flows from high to low, from top to bottom, but not this river…at least not twice a day! A side swell from the Severn bore runs up and up and up and stops just past Caerleon, beyond a stone hump-backed bridge. There, morning and evening, the world stops and holds its breath for a few seconds until gravity beckoning, the surge of water turns and starts to fall slowly back downward. Rilling and running, it follows its course til it merges with the Severn surge and flows seaward, as it was meant to do before diversion.

On this humpbacked bridge, where people gather to watch and experience the moment, on a certain afternoon, two people stand. He, tense-shouldered, nervous, trying to make casual conversation, betrays his tension with each foreshortened laugh, each sharp-shot sentence. *She* doesn't notice, so web-bound is she in the magic of the place. It is fabled that back beyond the mists of many seasons, the Round Table had been here, not at Camelot. A ruined Roman amphitheatre still squats beyond the bridge, row upon row of tiered stone seats. Legend says it was there the Knights encircled Merlin, equals as each were inscribed onto the pages of Arthurian myth. That's what she wants to see. But he lingers on the bridge, looking down at the water, *'I'm waiting for the exact moment'*, oblivious to the fact that she is eager for the romantic legend, not the bores pausing of time.

She, for her part, is equally oblivious that he carries in his pocket a gold circlet heavy with diamonds. He begins his question at the very moment the waters stand still, aware that her answer will affect the flow of the rest of his life. But she, hearing not him but the echoes of ancient chivalry, has already turned towards the end of the bridge, hurrying onwards and upwards towards the sign saying 'Roman Remains'.

A few seconds later, the waters stop their holding, turn, and being released, cascade downward, carrying his future in their tumbling.

Double Cross

-party music-

So glad you came.
I want you now!

Where's Moira?'

'Yet another conference!
I can't wait either!

Where's the birthday boy?

Running late from the office…

Again?!?

What beavers we married!!!

-text pings to each phone-

'Aloha
from us in Hawaii.
Poolside photos
and divorce papers
enroute.
Losers!!!'

The high heeled shoes

They live on the hall shoe rack, reflecting the inside and out, reality and façade of her life. Cobalt blue stilettos, a message to the world, shouting "I'm a professional, stylish, got-it-all-sorted kinda woman!"

The truth………..

She had fallen in love with his clarity of thought, his surety of the right thing to do, his stability. But in the twelve years since they married, the children she'd wanted had never arrived. They would have bent their dynamic with the fluidity which children cause by their very existence. He had become rigid, dogmatic, unyielding. Never physically hurtful, he now wounds with words. Intelligent and articulate, he knows exactly how to drive a dirk into her self-esteem, reduce her individuality, weaken her.

She walks through the house like an automaton, on red alert as she enters each room to check that all in it is just as he'd expect. His meals must be just what he likes, when he likes, served at the correct temperature. Clothes and sheets must be fresh laundered, feel and smell as he expects. Their marriage is barren in more ways than one - devoid of affection, empathy, and communication.

On a weekday morning however, chrysalis to butterfly, she transforms when putting on those shoes before leaving for work. Her shoulders lift, her chin rises, her eyes sparkle. In her office, she is the epitome of efficiency and professionalism. With the right greeting for everyone, she knows all the staff from doormen to secretaries.

"Your daughter's cold better, Zoe?"

"How's your back today, Joe?"

Each day she moves mountains from in-tray to out-tray. No client leaves her office dissatisfied.

Then it's time to go home.

There, closing the hall door behind her, she takes off the shoes, hangs up her working persona on a hook beside her coat. Someday, she'll change all this. She'll tell him she wants a divorce, but only when she's finished creating her new 'escape' life.

On that day, she'll also buy comfortable bright red sparkly sneakers

.... and she'll dance in them!

A Matter of Time

Read by the author on BBC Radio Ulster, 'Time of our Lives' programme, September 30th, 2018.
The guideline –'You must tell a true story from the past'.

They met at a dance, I was told, but not a dance as we would image it. Word would have been put out that two or three musicians would be gathering together in some house or other, on some night or other. Off they'd both have gone for the craic.

There he saw her - a single girl, slender, eyes sparkling as she birled past him, black waist length hair spraying out behind her. He knew of her that she was only eighteen. There she saw him -a single man, sturdy of frame, tight black curls like those of a baby lamb. She knew of him that he was forty-four.

They talked, each drawn to the other despite the age difference. By the end of the night, a meeting had been agreed. After that one, another and then another … until the families heard of it. One family said it wouldn't do, he was too old for her. The other family said it wouldn't do, she was too young for him. The two of them tried to see the sense of it, but their hearts made them deaf. They heard only the sound of their softly spoken words, the beat of the pulse in their blood.

On one prearranged evening, when there would be few attending the service, they went to the church. Afterwards, only two of the congregation remained, having stopped at the church door to gossip. They were asked to be witnesses… and the couple were wed. With a long look and a few private words, they parted, each to return to their family homes. However, overcome with the significance of what they were doing, they had underestimated the fact that the two women in the church had stayed to gossip. And a fine piece of gossip this was indeed! The two went round the houses as fast as their legs could carry them and their lips could spill the news. They started with the families.

It was a long evening, with everyone drawn together in the one house. Shouting from the families, silence from the couple. When all the emotion was spent, one inescapable fact remained. They were wed!

And so he took Mary Ann home to her wedding night in his farm up the Glen. That farm over the years saw the birth of nine children, sorrow at the death of three. It also saw the worry of the 'foot and mouth years' when they lost not one beast. Mary Ann had gone round every boundary rubbing the walls and fences with the most holy things she had, placing the farm in God's hands. It saw the comings and goings of the Second of the Two World Wars. Eventually the time came when it was right to leave the farm and move down to the cottage at the end of the loanan.

Mary Ann lived many more years in that cottage. The first time the age difference mattered was when he left her in his sleep at the age of ninety-two, and she was only sixty-six. A grandchild was appointed to live with her to look out for her safety. A new one was put in place when a grown one left the nest. She set her face to the west and waited for thirty long years until they met again. They are together forever now, in the family plot. It, like they, rests behind the Church at the foot of the Glen. The very same Church where my grandparents had followed their hearts… and wed.

Footnote -These are the facts as I remember them told to me. Others may prefer different facts. None of these may be the entire truth. This is simply ***my*** *story of my grandparents.*

Ampersand Seesaw

Black & white
Slave and Wasp

In & out
Old Etonians & uncloseted gays

Back & front
The nth last Rock tour & Pakis out!

Up & down
Home brewing & Last Orders please

Him & Her
Boris blamed & Sturgeon strained

Them & Us
Street wild youth & housebound seniors

Home & Away
Garden gossip & holiday flights

All & sundry
Community centres & slat-slipped homeless

Now & then
Mindful peace & sepia memories

Which One?

Shot through with exhaustion, she pushed open the door of the tiny two-up, two down behind St Pauls. They'd bought it in 1938, a time when it was still believed that avoiding war could be possible. Calling in favours after many weeks of double shifts at the factory, she'd cobbled together five days to go and see the boys near Hove. They'd been evacuated there nearly four years ago. Restricted services meant it took a full day travelling to get there and another to get back. The middle three days, however, had been so worth it.

'How they'd grown!'

That thought splintered apart at the sight of the two envelopes on the hall lino.

Freezing, she stared at them as if snake-like, they would bite her if she moved. Eventually the weight of her battered brown suitcase forced her to lower it to the ground. The paralysis of shock broken, she studied their fronts. One was standard Army issue, formal, impartial, an uninformative brown. The other was a rich cream colour, luxuriously soft to the touch, with her name and address written in public school copperplate. It must have been wet when they'd come to roost in her nest. The round date stamp on each envelope was blurred where raindrops had fallen onto the postman's hand. The damp spots had spread as they had lain on the lino in her absence.

Placing one on either side of the mantelpiece, she lowered herself into the chair at the fire. His chair. He'd last sat there on leave eight months ago during a too short long weekend.

"Nowt'll get me, lass. Don't fret, my love!", he'd reassured in his Yorkshire way.

The echo of that reassurance was lost in the deafening quiet of the two silent rectangles on the brown ledge. She rewound the last few days in her mind. She'd been so happy watching the boys building sandcastles and paddling, ruddy-cheeked in the sea air. Surely she'd have felt something if what she feared was true. If anything had happened to him, she'd have been heavier, clouded, pitted with sudden stabs of doubt. They were so close, so bonded! She'd have known!

She waited… thinking. Damn those blotched date marks! She needed to know which had arrived first. Senior officers wrote personal letters of condolence to those who had……. No! she was *not* going to think that. While she didn't know what was in them, her Bill was still out there somewhere, fighting away, determined to see the war out and come home to her and the boys.

The daylight from the street faded, no longer

fighting its way through the paper-taped windows. Still she sat on. Now in the cold dark, the outlines of the two rectangles were invisible but burnt on her mind's eye. She'd no idea how much time had passed before she decided which one to open first. Stiff with cold and inaction she stood up, checked the blackout was secure and lit the oil-lamp. In its flickering light , she forced herself to lift down the cream envelope and using a kitchen knife, carefully sliced it open. She might want to keep it for many many years to read and re-read.

Ignoring the greeting, she went straight to the next line on the single sheet of cream paper.

"I'm writing this on behalf of Bill, whose right hand is still bandaged after the explosion……"

Her vision became too blurred to read the information from the senior military doctor. The loss of three fingers on Bill's firing hand would render him no longer fit for active service as a sniper with his Regiment. On release from the Army Hospital in Normandy, he would be transferred back to Blighty. Due to the nature of his injury, he would be reassigned to one of the Regiments Quartermaster Offices. The page fell to the floor. Tears of relief spilled down her cheeks.

Backfire

You make no noise entering the cheap motel
room.
You reach the bed. They are oblivious.
The scar on his naked back moves rhythmically,
her red manicured fingernails curl in orgasm.

Bang!
Bang!
Not the sound a gun makes in films, you idly muse.

You see blood beginning to pool round your sturdy
sandals.
He had to die…leaving you for that tramp!
Your father's Army gun a useful legacy after all, you
smirk.
No! You're *not* sorry!

The pain in your side explodes.
As you crumple, one last angry thought.
'Damn, that bitch had a gun too'.

'The Slippers' by Samuel van Hoogstraten

The Threshold

(From the painting 'The Slippers' by Samuel van Hoogstraten)

Ginevra stands still in the hall, looking through the doorway to the parlour with the blue patterned tiles. She has been summoned.

"Immediately!" a servant had hissed, "The Master is waiting'".

Ginevra thinks wryly her father has indeed been waiting some time for this. He, her mother and Adrianus Janz will all be there, the weight of their conversation hanging heavy over the men, her Mother silent. Adrianus has come to ask for her hand - everyone knows that. Her father is eager to agree - everyone knows that too. An alliance between the two richest families in the Dutch East India Company makes sound economic sense.

Her father's dream of a son to inherit his company lie dead with the two small corpses in the family vault. He will never forgive Mother for bearing him three healthy daughters but two sickly sons. So, as the eldest daughter, it is expected that she will marry dutifully, a suitable son-in-law being the best substitute for a blood heir.

Here in this moment, at this threshold, she is merely a child of fourteen summers, a dependent, a pawn to be played by the Master at his whim, to suit his intrigues and plots. *Her* thoughts, wishes, dreams are of no importance.

Through that doorway is her future. The key players have been chosen. The script has been written. What might she make of her role?

She knows a little about Adrianus Janz. The Master has told her he is an astute trader, a widower in his early thirties, the only heir of his father, with a fine house on Weststraat. The servants have told her that he is short, plump, only slightly pock-marked and that he treats his own servants well.

Raised with more pragmatism than pride, she knows herself to be more than moderately pretty, generously proportioned, intelligent, and well trained in how to run a household. Many young Dutchmen have paid more attention to her at the Neuwe Kurk on Sunday than to the preacher, so she knows she has allure.

She considers.

Her eyes focus on the keys hanging from the door. They are normally attached to the belt around Mother's waist, the symbol of authority for any Dutch Mevrouw. They are the 'keys to the Kingdom' which is how any wealthy Dutch family regards their home- a kingdom, a refuge, a family sanctuary. It shows the state of Mother's mind that she has left them in the lock.

If Ginevra says yes in the room with the blue patterned tiles, she will then have her own realm to rule. She will hold the keys to her new home, to the cupboard of linens and fine tablecloths, to the chests of cinnamon and ginger, to the small box of precious Javan coffee. She will even have the tiny key to the huge family bible, displayed in the parlour of every successful Dutch merchant.

Her agreement will give her servants of her own to supervise in polishing the red floor tiles 'til they gleam, in washing the tiny glass panes in the long thin windows, in drawing up menus and stocking larders. She will give orders which will be obeyed, buy goods which will be delivered, be the head of the household when Adrianus is at the warehouse.

Then her vision sharpens…….

Adrianus will come home at the end of each working day. In the hall of his house on Westsraat, she imagines his over-slippers casually cast off, his cloak hanging from one of the hooks, other outdoor items discarded on the table. Further items of clothing will be cast off for comforts sake inside their home during the evening, until at last on reaching the bedroom each night.......

She deliberately closes the shutters of her mind.

She is no naïve child. She remembers last year when the scullery maid suddenly collapsed over the wash tub in the yard. Her cries of pain, the sudden rush of blood, the distorted scrap of flesh which emerged from her contorted body only to be wrapped up by Mother and thrown into the back furnace.

Try as she might to forget, she remembers Mother taking her aside later and the conversation which followed, as she was gently told of the workings of a woman's body and the realities of a marriage bed.

Again she looks at the doorway, then down at her feet. She stares at them wide-eyed as a child would. A candle on the table flickers out in a sudden draught. Unwittingly, her back straightens, her chin rises. With her eyes on the silver candlestick ahead, her right foot moves forward. With a fixed smile she enters the parlour.

There she faces Adrianus.

A summation of Seasons

Spring bounded in, almost knocking over his seat,
with a crocus smell of freshness, a bluebell dance in his step,
trailing hawthorn buds and part furled primrose leaves.
"Love me! I bring new sap and light and a promise of future joys".

Summer segued in, smoothly sinking onto her chair,
rosy cheeked, brightly attired, sun stretched like a garden cat,
a raindrop in her hair but perspiration on her upper lip.
"Love me! I warm you, unwind you, give you a time to make memories".

Autumn swept in, a swirl of russet leaves around her ankles,
looking lean, sinking into a cane seat in a miasma of mist,
dropping fruitful grains, berries and nuts onto the wooden floor around her.
"Love me! I bring the harvest, the riches of nature, a full fall of colour".

It's like walking a tightrope – Mary Farrell

Winter sliced in, silvering his seat with rime, rigid shouldered, well wrapped,
his shadow dark but his face blue-lit, body skeletal, breath steaming,
snow shiny, slush smudgy, a solidifying of movement once he'd sat.
"Love me! I clean the earth with death, preparing it for new life.

The Four sat drinking nectar poured by Nature,
toasting each other's elemental mystique.

Overheard

There for our usual lunchbreak in the graveyard of St Brides…on the bench under the weeping willow. Such a beautiful place in which to tell me you were leaving. Afterwards, during the waves of anger among my tears, I snidely thought that you'd set the stage with such appropriate props - the graves, the 'weeping' willow. Always the Drama Diva!

'An instant flare between us, we can't help ourselves', the words you used to sidle out of my life, tearing my world apart. She was beautiful, clever, rich - I learnt that later from so-called friends, who told me everything, delighting that my pain was not theirs. You left me looking like such a loser.

Years later, overhearing two women on the Covent Garden bus, I realize they're talking about you. I can't help eavesdropping…they have the raised voices of the entitled, one complaining to the other of the trial her brother-in-law has become.

'You know Owen lives with us now since my sister died. Our Christian duty to take him in. Deathbed promises and all that! At least his infirmity means he can feed himself, keep himself clean. But now

he's announced he prefers to work from home as an Editor. Says the busy City streets don't feel safe anymore. And really, our house is so big, and our housekeeper such a treasure. We have very little to do with him'.

Just as the bus stops for the Opera House, I hear, *'Now that he's totally deaf we don't take him out much. It's just too much fuss'.*

Her parting shot rises from the street below, *'He has more gin than hope these days'.*

***

Later, I muse over what I feel. Sorry, of course, for anyone jailed by the smug hypocrisy of that hideous woman. But the Dark in me whispers that you'd some such punishment coming.
I could find out where you live from old contacts in the Publishing House. I could visit to offer condolences on the death of your wife, the woman you deserted me for. I could sympathise with your deafness, recalling that early deafness runs in your family.
I could do all that.

But would my gift of a bottle of gin be given in sympathy or revenge?

Plenty of Fish

~the online angler ~

He cast his lure wide on the water.
He'd made it shiny, sparkling, intriguing,
a silver sheen glinting through its lines.
Adequate enough, he thought, used to easy past
success.
For long hours he sat, becoming marrow-chilled
through lack of heat or movement.
Not understanding, he stared at it swaying in the
waves,
willing it to dip, show nibbles of interest…
but not a single bite! It didn't tantalise.
His lugworm needed a shimmy of more
flexible movement, a core wriggle of liveliness,
to free it from an entrenched hook
of old-fashioned design. He didn't realise yet,
too set in his ways, he'd never reel in another fish.

Read at an Open Mic Session at Harrys Shack,
Portstewart, Autumn, 2019

Rescue Dog

Seeing Dreadlock Guy through the door of the community centre she freezes beside the hallway couch. In from her usual street spot under the archway, she shelters from the biting cold until they chase her out again. The Snake Logo on his jacket jerks a memory of the cold slither of his knife blade on her throat. Her trembling finger touches the scar he'd left the last time he was drunk. Her breath comes in short gasps. Shrinking behind the high back of the sofa she curls her body tight. Maybe he'll not see her!

Eyes widening in shock, she remembers Dog lying on the floor. Shaking hands drag the fleabag mutt round beside her. She tries to breathe up the nose of the shivering animal to calm it. Strange how she remembers to do that. Such a wisp of a memory from a long-ago TV show, watched when living with her father within the protection of four walls and a front door. It works. Dog seems to settle. She feels its heartbeat slow down, steadying. Bile stings her tongue and burns her throat. Fear makes her body heavy, pins her to the tiles.

The hunter in the street is triggered by some atavistic impulse. His head lifts, scenting the air, eyes darting around erratically. She knows he'll soon find her. Watching his head turning on his lizard neck - focusing, scanning, listening - a deeper fear than she has ever known breaks her paralysis. Dreadlock Guy can do what he wants to her, but he is *never* going to harm Dog. Dog needs to be protected.

She chooses her moment with care. Although every instinct screams *'Stay down'*, she grabs its skinny body and runs to the other end of the corridor where the orange sign says Toilets. Dog is heavy but unmoving in her arms. Throwing herself through the first door, then the second marked Ladies, she drops the animal to the floor. With shaky hands she tries to slam the bolt across. At first her fingers slip. Her gaze fogs with fear. She can't see the pin to grasp. Now the bile flows up her throat filling her mouth. Long fumbling moments later, she slides the bolt across, hearing the click. Her body sags, her spine dissolving.

Slumped on the floor, with Dog in her arms she repeats a mantra to steady them both.

"S' okay. S'okay".

Over the sound of her voice, angry thuds from the outside door filter through but they don't matter. She has done it. Dog is safe!

The McEnroe Dialogue

A woman in a bikini lies on a sun lounger beside a swimming pool. She is in her 50's, with bleached blonde hair and deeply tanned skin. Beside her on the edge of a chair at a metal poolside table is a man in his 60's, dressed in a golfing outfit. She is relaxed. He is tense.

*****

You cannot be serious!

Oh, cut the John McEnroe routine. Of course I'm serious….!

But she's more than half your age. Wait a minute, even less than that! She was at College at the same time as Janine. What on earth makes you think she'd look twice at an old goat like you!?!

Actually, she says she prefers older men!

There's older … and there's one foot in the grave!!! Now get real! Why do you want a divorce now anyway? You've been happily working your way through the office interns for years… with my blessing.

And why not? There was hardly a loving wife for me to come home to, was there?

Oh no!... you're not turning this round on me! We've had our comfortable understanding for years. Why're you going all ' I want a divorce' now? C'mon, out with it! What is different about this Michaela???

We're going to get married!

Marri...! You can't be serious. No, I'm not going McEnroe again. Just trying to get you to see sense! You know she could only be after your money! Does she know I'll get half of everything because of the Prenup? Not that that will exactly leave you short. Might have to sell a yacht or two, that's all! But I can't see why she'd actually want to marry you. You'd be stupid enough to give most of it to her anyway.

Just a minute, why wouldn't she want to marry me!?! I'm fit, interesting, urbane with a mature head on my shoulders.

Whaaa...! You use a golf trolley to go straight to the nineteenth, wouldn't know a Grand Master if it bit you, fall asleep during the News, get lost out of sight of Bel Air and your 'mature' head comes out of a bottle of Grecian 2000. Thanks to your father's Trust Fund, you've never done a proper day's work in your life. She must need a Sugar Daddy real bad if she's stooped to you. There's bound to be better bets she could flash her eye... or whatever... at. Mind you, she'd get them too! Fine looking young woman, intelligent, making a name for herself in the Cosmetics world, they say. WAIT A MINUTE! That's it! She's starting a Cosmetics firm, isn't she! She REALLY DOES want a Sugar Daddy! That's it, isn't it???

Well, I might have given her some financial help and advice.

Yeah right… cos you did! Or rather you gave her the money, and Rider and Sons gave her the advice… especially as Arnold Rider's the solicitor who drew up our Prenup.

Oh, let's cut this crap… a divorce or not?

Of course! I've nothing to lose. The kids have been waiting for it for years. They're too embarrassed by you turning up at every family occasion with a different floozie! Have your divorce. Get Arnold Rider on the case sorting out the papers… especially those concerning the financial split. Gimme my half… and Godspeed into the sunset with Michelle… sorry Michaela!

There's a slight catch!

Hmmm, thought there might be… or we wouldn't be havin' this conversation. Okay, spill!

Arnold has told me that for it all to be legal,

you have to see my next Prenup! It's part of the Trust. Goddam bastard of a father of mine wanted each wife to know the details regarding the next. Slimy ole git… as if he didn't have anything to explain when he left Momma!

Well, I can't say I ever warmed to him, that's true. But what's in a standard Prenup you mightn't want me to see!?!

In return for a half-share of my estate and income under California law, she's gonna give me a kidney!

Say what… say again! She's giving you a kidney in return for a half-share. Why not just buy one on the Deep Market?

Needs to be a decent match. The closer the match, the better chance of a graft working… and apparently my cousin Eulalia and her Dad… !

What!?! Not often you leave me speechless… but this sure as Hell is one of those times! Let me get this clear! You're distant blood kin. If she gives you a kidney as part of a Prenup, it's likely to be a better option than one from the open market. Sweet Jeez! You cannot be serious!

I've said before… enough of the McEnroe. A divorce or not… and without any more judgement!

Honey… I'm way past judgement! You should know that! If only I known your doctor's warnings about cirrhosis were more serious than you hinted... Hey, if this girl can give you what you need, nuff said! Start the divorce proceedings tomorrow! The kids have their own lives…and it's not as if it's something they haven't seen coming! By the way, feel I ought to say now. Luis Sanchez, our dog whisperer. He's giving me an corneal graft. I'm paying him plenty for it, as well as for training Mitzi…and for a few extra fringe benefits! He's using the money to bring his family to California. And seriously… would I have married you all those years ago if I'd known about my sight distortion!

Winter Solstice

The new moon scimitared a nightlong arc way
against a backdrop of black velvet, star shot.
Its light cast filters through the leaves
creating a reversed patchwork on the ground
of shadows and spaces, of dark shapes
batiked onto a gleaming puddle, shiny sheened.
A silhouette slithered its way on feline tiptoe
past the silvered rime on a frosted stone ditch.
The quick passing flash of a snowy owl was
fleetingly mirrored on his upturned dark retinas.
On this night of least light, of longest dwelling dark
the Universe stopped for a nanosecond
holding its breath in balance, until time moved on
and the dark reversed into light, and the night into a
longer day.

The cold light of day

On a last-minute whim, Jacob shoves the notebook into his pocket as he leaves the apartment. One of his Myriam's distinctive diaries. How he'd missed her this last year! Shuffling along the sidewalk, his arthritic hip complaining, he pulls his muffler tight around his neck against the chill of a New York winter morning. At first he just glances at a few words as he walks, wanting to see her familiar handwriting again. So uniquely sloping you had to bring the page almost horizontal to your eyes to make sense of it. As words and phrases slam into his consciousness, his steps slow until he stops altogether.

The impact of what he is reading hits his knees. Reaching the next street bench, old fashioned metal with peeling paint, he collapses. He can't go on to the shop now. His son Bernie would guess something was wrong. He feels dizzy, his body trembling, his throat dry and tight. Could he be having a heart attack? The notebook only a third full, he feels compelled to finish reading it all. Now. In one go. Okay, he'll be too late to open the shop, but Bernie will soon be there with his own set of keys.

Myriam had always written in notebooks even before they'd married. A familiar part of their life together, she writing while he read the Torah. Respecting her privacy, he'd never looked in the chest under the bed where the notebooks had piled up year after year hidden under blankets. She wasn't aware he knew about them but hey, he knew everything about his Miriam. He didn't need to look in them. They'd grown up together, families allied by race and religion. Their parents had decided they should marry at twenty, and he'd never regretted a moment of their forty-seven years together. He couldn't have hoped for a better, more devout Jewish wife and mother for their three children.

Diagnosed with leukaemia, she'd accepted it as God's will. Passing quietly and with grace, surrounded by their family in the apartment bedroom the two of them had shared for over forty years. Clearing out her things after the funeral, he'd been surprised to find the iron chest empty. He was even more surprised, a year later, to find this rogue notebook behind a box on a high dusty shelf. He'd been looking for a thicker scarf than his usual workday one. Instead, he'd found this. From the dates, it was her last one, written in those declining weeks before a rogue embolism had, without warning, stopped her heart before the cancer could.

His breath mists in the chilly air. A foot-numbing freeze from the icy sidewalk takes hold as he reads. He'd not bothered putting on his over-shoes that day - it was only a short distance from the apartment to the shop. Hadn't thought he would need them. But he also hadn't thought that he would be sitting here reading on a wintry street bench.

Words, phrases float out of the pages into the air above him. His mind strains to reach up and grab them, knit them into some alternative sort of sense. Isaac -his brother's name so often mentioned. The hardest punch comes from the words 'Bernie looks so like Isaac'. He wants to stop turning the pages but can't. Slow unheeded tears seep downward, some nestling in his wrinkled cheeks. Ignoring his mounting pain, he reads on. A bite as cold as the sleet-filled New York sky above him clamps his soul, as he learns that the scaffolding of his entire life has been a sham, a fakery.

Amor Fati

Today I saw a starling flitter
I remember golden eagles blazoning
through thermals in a heat-heavy sky.

Today I heard a seagulls' loud complaint
I remember cicadas, at dusk a swelling
Gregorian chant of chirped conversation

Today I smelt opening hyacinths
I remember luscious drooping passionflower,
the intoxication of sharp mint and sweet
honeysuckle

Today I tasted a store-bought stir-fry
I remember slabs of giant tomatoes, swollen with
juice,
drizzled with oil, counterpaned by white sheep's
cheese.

Today I felt an Atlantic wind waken my face
I remember the caress of a mountain breeze,
pine-laden, warm and gentle like a lovers' touch.

Today I am here…
but that was in another country
and besides, that wench is dead.

Footnote : Amor fati is a Latin phrase which may be translated as "love of one's fate". It is used to describe an attitude in which one tries to see everything which happens in one's life, including suffering and loss, as good or, at the very least, necessary. This piece is written to the Fates. The last two lines paraphrase both Christopher Marlowe and T.S.Eliot.

What choice?

Walking up to the farm Kate's sense of anticipation was high. What lay ahead this evening? Eamon seldom phoned her; he rarely saw any need. However, that morning in an unexpected call, he said he'd something to discuss when she called up as usual. Her mind kneaded at the dream she'd heartheld for so long.

They'd been an item for eighteen years now. It began when she was only twenty-three - a newly qualified district nurse, grateful for her first position in this tiny rural townland. So long ago it was still called 'courtin' then. Now forty-one, her biological clock thrummed out a loud drumbeat .

Biological clock- an easy phrase for people to say, for magazines to discuss, for the townsfolk to nod about and wink at her and jab her in the ribs with a knowing smile. They didn't know the pain of it, the constant aching like a stitch in her side. But who else was there but Eamonn? So many times she'd nearly broached the subject but stopped just short through fear of his reply.

But now- today - after eighteen years investment she knew what she deserved.

The pattern of their weekly meetings, too routine and devoid of any overt affection from him to be called dates, had started when his Ma was still alive, the only two of the family left living on the farm. Every Wednesday she'd go there, watch Corrie with Ma and afterwards put her to bed. Then she'd sit with him at the kitchen table, and over the oilcloth, he would say the same things week after week over tea and a slice of Battenburg cake. Lord, how she loathed Battenburg cake with its sickly pink icing and sugary pastel squares!

On Saturdays it was McMahons Hotel. In the early years, 'High Tea' had been served on linen tablecloths and willow pattern plates. Now eighteen years later it was called an 'Early Bird Special' after which there'd be drinks in the Private Bar. There every weekend the Malone brothers, with accordion and violin, would churn out the same tired come-all-ye's with monotonous regularity and little musicality. Afterwards, a quick walk to her door, a kiss on the cheek and he'd be home in time for Match of the Day.

Each Saturday night as she closed the door of her cottage behind him - and the months stretched into years - she'd think…'But who else is there?'. No-one in that area for sure… and that area was where she was steadily promoted, was professionally valued. She'd put down roots with the buying of the cottage, as District Nurse had brought many of the town's children into the world. She *had* to believe that any normal man would see sense eventually, would open his eyes to how much more she could add to his world, would realise how much richer his life could be.

McMahons Hotel held the heartbeat of that place if the town could have been said to have one. A time-warp hotel in the centre of a single linear street. Everyone went there for the appropriate meals for local Births, Deaths and Marriages. It was the accepted venue for weekly dinners, morning teas, committee meetings in the Upstairs Salon… and on Saturdays to catch up on the local news in the Bar while the Malone brothers droned on in the background.

It was in McMahons one Friday evening when it happened.

She was there with the three other district nurses from the area. Marie was leaving, going off with her fiancé to the city to be married and start a new life. All much younger than her, she felt she'd been invited only out of courtesy. After her usual two G&T s, on her way to the ill-lit door marked Ladies, her foot slid in a beer-spill stain. She stumbled, dropping her handbag. Seeing the contents sprayed out on the sticky floor, she was horrified.... not about what they showed but about what they didn't. Was this now her entire persona... brush, purse, keys! Nothing unusual, unique, individual.

She stared in shock, minutes passing, before she realised that the stranger from the nearest bar stool had picked some things up to hand back to her. Jolted into stuttering and stammering, she then became so tongue-tied she just stopped, was silent. Sensing her discomfort, among a litany of soothing statements he asked if she wanted a small brandy 'just for medicinal purposes'. Much to her surprise she heard her voice agree. Why ? Was she still in disgusted shock over the boredom of her handbag? Did she not want to go back to the excited conversation of the other nurses? Was she just longing for an anonymous face to talk to?

Whatever the reason- or maybe for all of them - she drank a brandy… and then another.

Conversation was easy. A Consultant Psychiatrist on his way to an annual convention, he'd taken a detour off the main road to stop for petrol, only to find the car wouldn't start again. It was just after 5.00pm. The single town mechanic had closed up shop. Could he stay overnight? It would be looked at in the morning as the mechanic was sure it was just the battery which needed replaced. Hearing the inflexibility in the suggestion, the Doctor had booked a room in the hotel. Finding himself at the bar on his own, whiling away time, he was as glad of her company as she was of his.

Afterward she used the brandy as an excuse. It may also have been his calm air, the way he cocked his head to one side when he was listening, really listening to what she said. She found herself, in piece by small shameful piece, telling him all about the tedious vacuum of her life. About Eamonn and the sham which was their romance - she actually choked when she said the word 'romance'. About his mother, her death, and the inheritance of the farm six months ago. All about the last eighteen years waiting, with her torturous inner clock ticking. Finally, about the tight control of her corrosive envy and wild rage when visiting the new-borns, the savage aching for one of her own. He seemed to understand, be sympathetic .

He was still sleeping the next morning when she let herself out of his room so early that no staff saw her escaping out the back through the kitchens. McMahons saw no point in starting their first breakfasts before 7:30am. Sometimes over the next few weeks she thought of him leaving that day, going onto his Convention and after it back to his wife, four children and comfortable, respectable life. She wanted no more than what he had given her - a different sense of herself, unfamiliar feelings, a new experience. That had been enough from him.

It was only two months later when she realised that the nausea each morning was both regular and indicative that she understood what a blessing he had given her. She held to her decision of not getting in touch. There was no space for the other in each of their lives. This baby was hers…and hers alone.

So tonight, when Eamon wanted to talk to her about something special, she went up to the farm with two pathways clear in her mind. Was he going to say something of importance? … which would fast track to a church aisle, a white dress and a prematurely born baby, or so everyone would think. Or would it be just another unimportant piece of news which he mattered in his world but meant nothing to her?

Well, if that was it, within the coming week she'd hand in her notice, pack her car, withdraw her savings, and move to the city. As an experienced nurse, she'd always find work and be able to make a nest. There she would wait alone with contented anticipation for the arrival who would restore her heartbeat.

Today's Special

Wind-blown, he's hurled through the café door into a world of breakfast smells. Scanning the Menu Board on the wall, his stomach churns. Focused by hunger, he sees nothing else.

Alone in the corner she pats her curls, re-swathes her scarf and stares at him with shining eyes. Alone at the window the other re-opens her paper at the already completed crossword. With pen poised and a fetchingly furrowed brow, she stares outside as if for inspiration.

After ordering, he chooses a single table at the door. Shoulders sagging, in sync, the two women sip cold stale coffee.

A la Munch

Standing cliff-edge, knife-edge,
she screams out to sea.
France won't hear
her anguish.

Why?

The need to know.
He jumped off
Beachy Head.
That's what's done
at the point of no return.
Flailing down rockward
he left her voided.

What now?

A futile future.
Churning anger fills
the space.

Why not her too?

An autobiographical Tale – Performed on the Stage at a Tenx9 event, October 2019

Tenx9 is a storytelling event where nine people have up to ten minutes each to tell a true story from their own life.

I was delighted when my friend Anne agreed to tour Italy with me during my first student summer holiday. Anne was golden olive of skin and rounded in a most voluptuous Sophia Loren way. She was also blessed with long jet-black hair which fell to her waist in a thick mesmerizing swaying. I was the exact opposite- pale, skinny and of Celtic hue. Nuff said! Ten minutes after leaving the plane in Rome airport, I realized I'd become invisible as a group of young Italian stallions encircled her, vying to touch the hems of her bell-bottoms. Truly the entire Jenner clan - every last K of them - wouldn't have stood a chance had they been living at that hour!
That formed the pattern of our Italian trip …
but there was one time when I was centre-stage, and the limelight was all mine!

Staying in Naples and, having visited Pompeii, we decided to take a bus tour to see Vesuvius. Naively we thought that the bus would drive to the top. There we'd stand on viewing platforms to admire and photograph stunning views of the Bay of Naples. My first hint of worry began when the bus pulled up at the collection point. Being cash-tight students, we had of course chosen the cheapest tour, but this vehicle was a revelation. It looked like something the Scooby-Doo gang had used until it fell apart. Choking and spluttering, the rusty little minibus began the slow perilous crawl up the countless S-bends to the top. My whimpers grew louder with every crashing of gears. At every treacherous curve the bus would pause, hold its breath before deeply inhaling and then would bravely resolve to go onwards and upwards. At each pause, in my mind's eye we'd lose purchase, and start to career backwards down the slope gaining momentum until we'd concertina into a tightly smashed wreck at the bottom. Eventually I just shut my eyes and resigned myself to a fast reverse into oblivion.

Finally, we shuddered to a halt. I think I heard a piece of metal crash to the ground somewhere at the rear. I couldn't be sure as I was so busy singing Halleluiahs and fighting to be the first passenger off the bus. It was only as I stood on Terra Firma that I realised that the truly terrifying part of the journey was just about to begin. The minibus had brought us up the skirt of the mountain, but we had to go still further and climb the cone of the volcano.

And this was to be done by ski lift! If I hadn't been rendered speechless, I'd have objected, but I think

I temporarily lost consciousness through fear. By the time I was compos mentos again, I found that Anne and I had been strapped into two iron seats on the chairlift. These looked like rejects from a Fairground Wheel abandoned since the St Louis State Fair of 1904. With much creaking we began to move upwards, Anne smiling and swinging her feet. No, of course there was no footrest! I on the other hand, realised that only a thin leather strap prevented me slithering out of the chair altogether. I began to mentally reel through my few worldly possessions wondering who would claim what on my inevitable demise.

After a time, as we moved upwards and over the surface of the steep cone, in a macabre sort of way I decided to study it. I wanted to see the last thing I would feel as I hit the surface and began to die. The cone was covered in a fine brownish coloured grain, with all the consistency of a Saharan sand dune. Nothing to grasp or hold on to. If the fall from the ski lift didn't kill me, the hurtling slide down the cone would. I passed through fear into some kind of mindless disassociated state. As a result, when we reached the top, I allowed myself to be catapulted out of the chair. I landed, *not* on a carefully constructed viewing platform, but instead on a slippery strip of volcanic earth about nine feet wide, without railings or a steady surface underfoot. On one side of this strip was the nine hundred foot drop we'd just ascended by ski-lift. On the other was a six hundred foot drop straight into the volcanic core at the bottom of which we could now see the flames of Hades.

My body froze, rigid… rock… still, buffeted by the arriving visitors who pushed past me, rushing like lemmings to the rim. I distinctly remember two German ladies - of course, they were used to Alps! - getting down on their knees and dangling by their toes from the edge. They were eager to get a suitably clear photograph of the potential Crematorium below.

The man who ran the ski lift had evidently come across my like before. Clicking his tongue angrily he pointed at the only thing on the volcanic rim - one solitary boulder about six feet high and ten feet in circumference.. Picking me up in my rigid pose like a Madame Tussauds waxwork he clamped me to said boulder, my face into it and my arms outstretched limpet-like around its girth … and there he left me.

By now I was resigned to my inevitable end. In my head I began to list all the things I'd now never do, a bucket-list in reverse. I'd just started with 'I'll never go to another Student Disco' which
was, in hindsight, a strange prioritizing of unaccomplishments in a life cut tragically short when my fingers touched something on the other side of the boulder. Looking round it, there peering at me was a little woman, similarly limpeted to the other side. Determined in my final moments to be polite, I

stammered a few words.

"Hello, I'm Mary, who are you?"
"I'm Maggie and I'm frae Belfast"

The Universe had done us proud; we were going to shuffle off this mortal coil in the company of a fellow country woman.

;

But no! I'd underestimated the Italian nation. Just as I was about to learn more about my fellow coffin mate, with a rush from behind, I was enveloped from head to waist in a smelly hessian sack. Like someone being kidnapped, I was carried sack-bound to the chairlift where I could hear metal clips attaching me to the chair belt and to a person in the adjoining seat. A male voice spoke Italian in my ear. Feeling the chair moving slowly downwards, my chief fear this time was not that I'd fall but that I'd suffocate in the tight sack. My panic deepened when my head and shoulders were enveloped by a surrounding arm, pulling me into the side of my fellow ski-lifter. One of my major life lessons has been that there are few more distinctive odours than the armpit of a middle-aged Italian male who doesn't wear deodorant. I tried to breathe through my mouth, both to save oxygen and to keep out the unique smell .

After a light-headed eternity, the downward movement stopped, the ties were released, and the sack was removed. I looked into the leering, unsavoury face of a man who had obviously thoroughly enjoyed the whole encounter. I could not say the same! but I was distracted by the realisation that I was now going to live.

Anne and I travelled down the mountain again in the minibus, but it no longer held any fear for me. I had faced death, and it had not claimed me. I have never since climbed another volcano; I *did* go to another Student Disco.... and with all my heart I sincerely hope Maggie is not still up there with the rock. I hope she went on, post-sack, to lead a full and happy Belfast life.

Thank you.

Scene from a window

-by Bella Rochester at Thornfield Hall -

How dare she! Looking up at him with those doe eyes, she with her homely face, dowdy clothes and scraped back hair! I see them down there, as I look through the narrow window, she holding the child's hand. The child seems to like her, gurgling and laughing and burying her face in those drab skirts. When he appears, in play, to chase and roar and tease, the little chick runs to her for safety.

And him! for pity's' sake, what has she for him? Not like me! When he first saw me, he called me his bird of paradise. I dipped and danced and glided around him with my sun-tinted skin, flowing black hair, tiny waist, and the lilt of my song. So enchanted he was, so spellbound, visiting for longer and longer each day.

He was grateful for any brief minutes of my time which I carelessly threw his way. A coy smile, a flutter of my fan, the faintest touch with just the very tips of my fingers. The gossamer of my web tendrilled him without him even knowing, until he was tight bound, desirous only to be at my side forever.

My brother would sidle in, with whispers of

dowries and warnings of other suitors which led to that one gloriously bright Caribbean day. The church gaudy and swollen with guests, the colours and scents of frangipani, hibiscus, passionflower, and rich white orchids, as I floated up the aisle in my wedding finery. That day, oh how he plighted his troth, with adoration and the pain of wanting and the joy of getting. What a treasure he had won. I saw the victorious joy in his eyes!

But then back here to Thornfield. My feathers have become soggy and bedraggled in the rain, the glow of my face has faded under dark rain clouds and my beauty is misted over for him.

I am caged in this room, a broken bird exiled from her paradise. When I look out the window, how dare he have that same soft look I know so well but now for her, that brown timid sparrow! I try to sing through the window once more for him, my Rochester, but he hears only her, that little plain Jane.

All Hallows Eve

shadow fingers creep
  shades cascade from
    a scudding moon
     to blur
       obscure

shapes shimmer into horror
  the night terrorises as
    known becomes unknown
      bewildering
        flickering

light loss
  night gloss
    over a land alien now
      dark with unholy dreams

things go bump
  wings thump
    with irregular beat
      echoing an unsteady heart

time is ajar
  with an hour

lost

It's like walking a tightrope – Mary Farrell

Secret Attic Magazine:- Picture This! Challenge , June 2021
Using the picture, write a story of no more than 1000 words

The Cracking of the Mirror

'Wunderkind' the press had called him. How the paparazzi would love to see him now! He imagined the tabloid front pages. Hiding in a booth in a side-street eatery! He'd ignored his sixth sense jangling lately. Now after just a few short phone calls… !

His meteoric rise had made headlines in the financial world. With an instinctive nose for over-extended companies about to crash, he'd buy them for a song, break them up and off-load the smaller units at great financial gain. The moniker no-one used to his face was 'The Spare Parts Dealer'. His business team was nicknamed 'The Foxhounds', eager as they were for both the hunt and the kill.

His personal life too had had a successful upward curve. From a Council Estate in Barnsley, a scholarship to Oxford had smoothed out his accent. Marrying Louise, the granddaughter of an Earl, a month after his graduation, brought him connections with both the Tory Party and the English Peerage. The Company he then founded was sleekly promoted by her brother's PR firm. Assuming in turn the labels of millionaire, multi- and then billionaire, an amicable divorce re-allocated his assets and their three children to everyone's satisfaction. Louise got the children and the Cotswold estate and he the South Bank penthouse.

Oiled by his annual profits, his years passed comfortably. Saint Moritz in January, Rio at Easter, his Bahamian holiday home in August, and Australia each November for the Melbourne Cup. The backdrop to a satisfying London life. He regularly featured in the media with this season's mistress, each as beautiful and intelligent as the last. He had the usual entourage of housekeeper, cook, and personal trainer as well as Season tickets for all the appropriate events both cultural and sporting. His Private Accountant and Personal Secretary were as discreet as they were efficient. His life purred smoothly.

Until Monday morning. Only yesterday!

Arriving at the office, he was surprised to find Elaine's desk unoccupied. His Personal Secretary had been there at 8.30 sharp every morning for the last fifteen years. Disconcerted he nonetheless began his day by ringing Charles, his Accountant, but was told that he too was not at work yet. How very curious! Speculation about this was interrupted by a call from his Chief Investments Banker. Why had he cancelled the monthly funding for the Coral Project? As he had done no such thing, he ordered the banker to his office immediately. A subsequent investigation revealed a long list of similarly cancelled payments. Over the weekend, the funds for them all had been diverted to a Cayman Island account.

The afternoon brought more bad news. Huge deficits appeared right across the wide band of his investments and bank accounts. The revelations continued long after business hours. After far too few hours' sleep, he spent the morning with four different Bank Managers trying to quilt together a patchwork of borrowed funds to disguise the extent of his financial disarray.

Just before noon he phoned Louise. She would understand and help. She was indeed sympathetic but explained that all of her available assets were tied up in the various business ventures of their children. And there was certainly no point in approaching the children she went on to warn him. After all, he hadn't helped them with any initial funding for *their* businesses when asked, lecturing them instead on self-sufficiency!

By mid-afternoon his pride could no longer stubbornly insist on ignoring that the disappearance of both Charles and Elaine yesterday had a related significance. As the skein further unravelled, it had become clear that his two most trusted employees - whom he considered his close friends!- had combined their knowledge to betray him. Charles had indeed been one of his best assets. No-one could even begin to follow the money trail; the tracks were so cleverly hidden. Over the weekend, they, and most of his money, had vanished without trace.

By close of business, he realised he'd barely eaten for two days. Booking a table at a down-market restaurant where he would be anonymous, he left a voicemail for Chrissie, his latest mistress, to meet him there. He left the office building by the back entrance. Maybe he was being paranoid, but he could swear he saw some reporters in the Front Lobby. To be inconspicuous he took a taxi to 'Fusion'. Sliding into a back-booth, he ordered food, and an exceptionally good Chardonnay. He was in deep trouble, yes, but he could still turn this round. He knew he could!

He poured a glass for Chrissie. He needn't have bothered. A short phone-call informed him that she would not be coming. Elaine had phoned her on Sunday night, hinting that she seek out another benefactor. A handsome Italian high-flyer in the City had been very welcoming last night when she'd moved from the apartment which *he'd* rented for her into Ernesto's new townhouse in Chelsea. Yes, she and Elaine *had* become remarkably close over the last few months. He hadn't known? He'd never asked!

He stared at the cooling food on his plate…thinking. When the phone rang again, he was tempted to ignore it, but a fatalistic curiosity took over. Yes, this was he. Whose office? Dr Fisher in Harley St?

but he'd had his routine medical check last week for the Insurance Company. The full works - blood test, x-ray, even a sight and hearing test. The results? Sorry but he was too busy to attend to routine test results at the moment. What! Could you repeat that please?

As he put the phone down with a shaking hand, an unfamiliar sensation uncurled behind his eyes. Without warning, tears began to stream. When actual drops began to fall onto his place mat, he covered his eyes with a pristine Henry Poole linen handkerchief.

Even those born without a silver spoon but who fight hard to buy one, should never doubt the ability of the Fates to decide who keeps it!

At the Fork

His lungs laboured with deep gasps as he ran, hearing behind him excited yelping. On the forest floor, the footsteps of the dogs' owner were more muted but still too close. Isaiah knew he shouldn't have looked at the tray on the windowsill, but the smell of baking had sucked him through the trees, up to the house, right to the very sill. His stomach had spasmed with hunger at the thought of fresh bread.

Who's there? Get away from here. Where's my rifle, Flo?

Ah, Caleb, I don't know. Where you left it fore coming to bed.

Someone's out there spying on us! You sure your man's gone hunting all weekend?

Course I'm sure! Or you wouldn't be here. C'mon back to bed, a little more fun and then we'll eat.

Nah! I saw someone. Gotta be sure they saw nothing, or your Homer'll do for us. Ah, there's my rifle. You let out the dogs!

Isaiah ran for his life, back out through the trees, knowing he'd leave a trail. At the fork, which way should he go? The left had no signs of use, the right showed footprints in the mud. Did the left go nowhere, the right somewhere with people? 'More people' flashed like lightning in his brain. He chose the right path. Nearly four hundred tiring footsteps later, he collapsed behind a tree root and lay there panting. A shadow blocked his light. A mountain of a man stood there, carrying a rifle and three blood-stained sacks, some stains stone dry, others sweating fresh red.

You're a skinny little one, aren't you? Running hard too. You hungry? Well, how about you help me with these sacks, they're getting real heavy. And we'll talk back at my place where my wife Flo'll feed us both.

An Abecedarian Conversation

-A Bronx Boss and his Secretary -

All the money's gone?
Bank accounts completely cleaned out.
Can you believe that!
Didn't deserve this, did we?
Even if we were having an affair…
For f****s sake, we were discreet.
Gotta accept they found out.
How?
I'm not psychic!
Just think, how?
Kept the Motel assistant sweet, didn't I?
Little s***, think he blabbed?
Might have.
No other way they could've found out?
Only Credit Card receipts.
Private account used though.
Quite a clever ruse, I thought!
Really good one… I thought so too.
Smart yeah... but not smart enough.
They *did* find out, that's true.
Underhanded of them.
Very devious!
Well, they're both gone now… with all the money.

Xmas at my house then?
You think I'm staying with *you* now !?!
Zero chance of anyone else...now we're both b
r
o
k
e!

A second chance for us then?…
But this time openly.
Can we though?
Do you want to?
Enough!!!

FFS! Can't we just talk normally!?!

Footnote:- An Abecedarian piece of writing is one in which the first letter of each successive line of writing follows in alphabetical sequence.

Wind turbines on a May afternoon

Propellers, swish-scything down a bright breeze,
sleek shaped in windmill circling,
o'erlook the fairy ring, which, hawthorn hemmed,
embeds the May magic of ancient spells.
A solitary sycamore centred in the Rath below
vies to impress but its symmetry is outshone
by troupes of purple bluebells, dancing playful
in sunbeam spotlights, sifted by cloudwisp.
Sheep cluster and bleat, cows drift
from tuft to tuft, hides stroked by breeze-fingers
which scatter the flies, dispersing their divebombs.
Two cuckoos cry a double echo, impossible to source
in the greenland - tree, bush, and shrub - under the
wide sky.
The horizon fades into a heat-haze which ripples sight.

Only children

easy to recognise -
the over achievers
the compromisers
the pleasers

weary of being misunderstood
you can have my family
the whole bloody lot of them
such a careless throwaway
of a Holy Grail
or
weren't you the spoilt one!
but toys and coins
don't play
or laugh.

terrapins lacking shells
supersensitive
hitting the rocks in
social chitchat
the workplace
with lovers and friends
hiding flinches
from unintended stings.

It's like walking a tightrope – Mary Farrell

we take words and people
at face value
unfamiliar with power plays
for position
no other manoeuvring cubs
in the litter

untrained in the ring of
yes, you do look fat in that
and
I get more cos I'm better

the toughening tumble of sibling banter
is replaced by the full weight
of family expectations.

Yes, we recognise each other.

A Tale of a Barn

Winner of the Lurig Drama Club Competition, 2021
Read by the actor Ciaran Hinds, November 26th, 2020 @ www.thenineglens.com

They said he shouldn't have settled there. It was too remote. The barn was too rundown. The neighbours were too few and far between. But he hadn't been able to resist the ruin at the head of the Glen. Snug in the shelter of oak trees, its gap-toothed door, jauntily hung on one hinge, had smiled at him. Ferns behind empty windows had winked at him. Uneven walls had flirted with him from behind fans of high nettles.

In his lodging house at the seashore that morning he'd challenged himself to walk the Glen from bottom to top. As he moved upward so did his heart. The land's curve would not have changed since his grandparents had been born here. Birdsong speared the air with darts of pleasure, bluebells rang out a welcome and a soft Spring dew silvered the grass tips. By the time he reached the ruin his legs were tired, but the sights and smells of the trenches had retreated before the peace which lapped at the Glen top.

Leaving at first light, he'd brought sandwiches and a bottle to fill at the burn which rilled and ran and tumbled along the Glen floor. As he ate, with his back against a smooth-stoned wall, sun-warmed and sturdy, he drank in the sides of the Glens arcing towards each other, melting in a patchwork of greens. Field green, hedge green, tree green, grass green all sown up in a shimmering hem in the distance where sky-blue melded with sea-blue. Buzzards hung lazy in the air, drifting where the thermals nudged them. Butterflies danced over bushes, toying with the idea of landing. The smell of wild garlic blended with the delicate scent of hawthorn, and the burn sang a song of past snows and spring rains and the joy of flowing. For the first time since he left the battlefields, his soul began to slow and be still. The next morning, he began the process of buying and restoring the barn.

His plans unambitious, he did most of the work himself. One room with a fire for daytime and one with a bed for night time - that was the spine of his home. A loft for storage, a byre for a few animals, and a stone store built over the burn to keep food fresh, that was enough for his physical needs. Add to that a wooden bench outside the door for summer, a comfortable chair by the fire for winter, and a black and white sheepdog constantly at his heels.

In the evenings, after a day on the hills with the sheep, or in the potato field, or among the growing vegetables, he would sit and allow himself to think. Increasingly, in the way you'd touch a sore tooth with your tongue, he'd prod open the cage around his thoughts, nudging it wider and wider as the months passed. The other men had died. He had not. Why? He had carried this heavy burden since France. An only child, his parents died in a house blaze when he was four. Grandma had raised him until tuberculosis defeated her in that long-ago August when war was declared. One of the first to leave in the troop ships from Belfast, no one in the crowd cheered just for him. Yet he had survived all those years, with only one leg wound on the second day of the Somme, one small external battle scar. He remembered their desperate superstition –'Stick with Eoin, he's a lucky charm'. And indeed, his luck had lasted! But not theirs.

No luck for the ill-taught, whose letters from home he'd read out loud so many times. Nor for the shattered bodies who'd slid down from the trench top, blood smearing. Or the tattered corpses hung for weeks on the barbed wire fences, ever shrinking. But him ! he was still here. Why? kept echoing. A question he couldn't answer and in the beginning had not even been able to ask. Only after many months in the barn at the top of the Glen could he even let it slither into a crack in his mind, and then he began to remember their faces. And those of their families! Where was the sense! He'd had no-one to grieve for him, save a handful of cousins in Cork. He couldn't face the wives, the mothers, of those who had died. Their eyes accused him. They denied it, but he knew better. His shame was corrosive and deep.

One morning, some two years after he'd moved in, Eoin lifted his head and looked around him. Really looked! Not at the land, he knew that well enough. But at the few roofs he could see. They said he'd no neighbours close, and for the most part that was true. But there was a back way to the McCleans - across the burn, up the bluebell wood, follow the line of the next two fields on the ridge top and then down the loanan - which meant they were only fifteen minutes away. They'd welcomed him when he'd first arrived and saw him settled in, but then respected him enough to leave him be. They hoped that, like an ill-treated dog, he would in time heal enough to seek out human company.

Carrying fresh laid eggs, new potatoes, and a clutch of wild fennel, he took the shortcut to the McClean farm. Five souls lived there – John, his wife, his mother, and his two sons. A great fuss was made of him, tea was served in the best cups and a fresh currant loaf intended for tea was sliced early. Work was paused and the whole family took part in a conversation of welcome. When Eoin revealed that he could play the mouth organ a little, he was invited to call any Saturday evening. The McCleans had an open door then, welcoming all visitors, especially those who could entertain. He stressed his poor playing, but the point of these evenings was for neighbours to come together. Being there at all, he'd fulfil that purpose. His musical skills didn't matter. When he left, it was in a flurry of overlapping sentences about the coming Saturday, which he'd promised to attend.

But things turned out differently as they sometimes do. By eight o clock the following Saturday, nine adults arced round the McClean hearth, some to sing, some to play. Each was enjoying the craic, when Eoin gave in to an impulse to repeat a story Grandma had often told him - a tale of hawthorns and fairies, of disrespect and consequences. And as he told his tale, the gathering stilled, breath was held, and movement stopped as his gift became obvious. He was a natural teller of tales, his words weaving and curling in the air, binding his listeners with strands of enchantment. On finishing the first, another was asked for, and another.

And so, the pattern was woven. Each week he'd garner some tales, from his memories of his grandmother, or books he'd read, or people he'd met, and each week more and more would climb the Glen to hear them. Soon the McCleans had to move the gathering outside - around a bonfire in summer, and into their newly built barn in winter, circling a brazier of glowing coals. The listeners provided both the materials for the new barn and the energy to build it… and also each week food and drink, wood and charcoal. Eoin sewed his magic into the circle and coaxed tales out of the visiting story tellers. For the news of these nights had spread and many wanted to listen… and to tell… and to be lifted into other worlds, their real lives suspended. As for Eoin, this became his real world. For this he became known throughout the Glen.

At last, he was able to put down his burden as his future became one of many tales with many different endings.

Where is the Author Now?

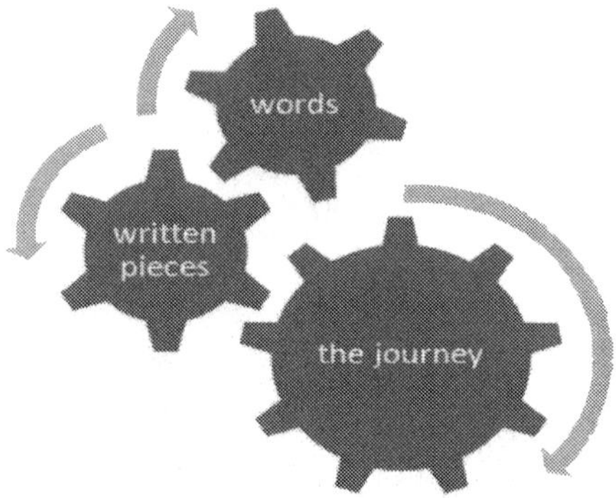

So where have all these 'Tightrope' Acrobatics led the Author?

Beginning this journey in the Spring of 2017 , by the summer of 2021 she finds herself now most comfortable writing Short Stories. To date, she has completed a Trilogy of sixty short stories - three groups of twenty intertwining tales, each section set in a different time and geographical zone. However, all three collections have the same feel in the way in which the characters connect and interweave in each set of twenty tales. The overall emphasis is on the individual, and the universal issues and struggles which everyone may experience.

Using the same format, she has recently begun another series of twenty short stories called 'The Street'.

On the following pages you will find the Prologues of each of these Collections.

The Kingdom

Prologue

Made up of hills and valleys, it was not a large kingdom. The land was rich and green, its curves soft and blending, bordered on one side by the sea and on the other by low mountains. Over time, the inhabitants had developed their own ways and customs, not too dissimilar from those beyond the mountains, but different enough to be distinctive. They felt a kinship among themselves, like an echo deep in their birthing. To those outside the borders, they appeared fey, with an ability to connect with the unseen, a way of doing things which were not always explainable, an extra layer of knowingness. Those who lived there were not aware of this, thinking themselves to be just as normal as those foreigners whom they met in the markets, or when they travelled to other lands. And yet it was there, deep in them but rarely surfacing, like a waft in the breeze or notes faintly heard from a pipe far away.

They lived their lives, as people do,
with their share of joys and woes, curiosities and
celebrations, and the comfort of routine.

And these are some of their tales.

Maybury

Prologue

Maybury was a place with an identity crisis. It didn't know whether it was a village which had stretched or a town which had stayed small. In the Domesday Book, it was listed as Meretun, with a bridge, a market, a manor house, a church, 16 households and a priest. It sat sleepily in its surrounding countryside until the Voting Reform Act of 1832 when it was proposed that it be renamed Mereborough. For practical reasons and ease of writing on maps and in official documents, this became Maybury. By then 348 souls resided there. Bypassed by the railways and the main roads north, and having no major industry, by the last Census the population had reached 1,402. It still had a bridge over the small river, now called the River May, and a thrice extended Church with a sundial dating back to 1782. It also had a High St, a primary school, the 'Horse and Hounds' pub and an array of small streets and lanes which had grown up around the Green. There were two housing estates, one begun in 1934 by the Government and the other in 1955 by a local builder. Its small shops and one supermarket were supplemented by the surgeries of a doctor and vet. There was a small community hall. The Library Van came once a week. What couldn't be found in the local shops could be bought in the nearest town twelve miles away, accessed by a regular bus service.

It's like walking a tightrope – Mary Farrell

What more could its inhabitants need?

The place catered for their souls, minds, and bodies.

But what of their emotions?

Ah, for that you'll have to look at the following stories.

And so Reader…..

Welcome to Maybury.

New Asgarth

Prologue

One of the first Domed Cities, it was now showing signs of age. It had been built in a hurry, with the more primitive technologies available at the time. Survivors had needed shelter quickly, so the actual Dome had been the priority and little thought had been given to daily life there and the needs of a community. The site chosen was near what had been the city of Billings, Montana. The worst of the damage after the bombs and the subsequent Radiation Waves had been mainly in a band around the Equator, bringing devastation and death to Central Earth. Further north and south from the Tropics of Cancer and Capricorn, evidence of destruction became less and signs of life increased. The old Montana was far enough north for Fourth World life to be sustainable there.

The bulk of the human race now lived in the north of the globe, with a few other small pockets in what had been southern Australia, New Zealand and the tip of South America. While in time ruined buildings could be rebuilt and some technologies reclaimed, the worst damage had been from the Radiation Waves. Population figures were decimated, but the impact on global animal, insect and plant life had longer lasting implications for the future. Animals and birds which survived were now declared 'Endangered' and while they could provide milk and eggs, they could not be eaten. Plants which survived in radiation-free areas were carefully cultivated and eaten only if they would reproduce again the following year. As a result, food was of a limited variety and carefully rationed.

Life in a Dome was harsh and uncomfortable. Zones were drawn up for Production, Health and Care, Education and Training, and Habitation, and given that order of priority. The three-story apartment blocks of New Asgarth were built using baked clay and the remains of any ruins nearby. They were furnished with what could be salvaged or recycled. Moving around was mainly by walking, although a select elite were allocated bicycles. A few reconstructed vehicles were reserved for High Council members and the Military. Food was distributed weekly from Rationing Stations. A Black Market in goods flourished, but the concept of paper money had dissolved with the bombs.

Although Dome life was hard, people had heard of the Scroungers, bands of renegades who preferred to take their chances in the war-ravaged Exterior Lands rather than submit to a life strictly controlled by the Dome Authorities. Therefore, survivors preferred to fight the familiar problems inside the Dome -rationing, vermin, stale air and water, etc - rather than the unknown threats of life outside the Main Gates.

At first, the World Council in Stockholm had decreed that Domes should be permanently shut against any remaining radiation. Cities in the far north had gradually abandoned this idea as the air there, over time, proved to be contamination free. The City Council of New Asgarth however was unconvinced of this, and their Dome remained closed, leaving the city air stale and unpleasant.

How did the city get its name? One of the few artefacts which survived intact after the bombs of the Great Conflict was a statue of an early gold prospector of the 1800s. The architects liked this emblem of the triumphant survival of the human race and its history, and thus the city was named after the engraving on the plinth - A.S.Garth.

The Street

~ Prologue ~

The building of the original street was finished in 1838, and thus it was called Coronation Street. On moving in, its first inhabitants celebrated beginning a new life for themselves, as well as the reign of the new Queen. Three-storied, red bricked, and spacious for their time, the houses were bought by middle-class Victorians to flaunt their comfortable social status. With the street's proximity to the centre of the then town, the short daily journey to office or business was possible by foot. The communal gated garden in front catered for nurses with perambulators, wives who wanted afternoon strolls and gossip, and children who needed a safe arena in which to play with dolls, cricket bats or in which to re-enact military victories.

Time marched on. The garden rails sported black ribbons at the Queen's death and colourful bunting to celebrate the ending of two World Wars. By the time the street was ready to welcome yet another century, the City Council decided to honour it with a new name. The signs now read Millennial Avenue. Those over a certain age continued to refer to it as Coronation Street, despite frequent cliched referrals to a certain soap opera. Those in their twenties and below tended to refer to it by its new nickname, Milly Street.

Today the street has a very different facade. Despite showing the wear and tear of nearly two centuries, the gated garden and a few of the buildings have remained for the most part unchanged. Many of the others have been divided into three flats. The ground floors of some have been converted into social or business premises. The street now has a Community Hall, a launderette, and a shop at one street corner with a pub at the other. As it is to the east of the City Centre, some people enjoy pointing out that it now resembles the set of another popular soap opera much more than the one suggested by its original name.

The inhabitants of Milly St live their lives with less drama and more authenticity than any actors on television, but their characters, interactions and scripts are no less interesting.

Read on… and make some new friends!

About the Author

Born in the Glens of Antrim, Mary Farrell has spent much of her life living on the North Coast of Northern Ireland. After 26 years teaching 11-19-year-olds and two years as an Advisor with the Northeast Education and Library Board of Northern Ireland, she lived in the foothills of the Pyrenees in S.W. France for six years.

For the last three years she has been a Facilitator of two Creative Writing Groups in Northern Ireland, known collectively as the North Coast Writers Group. During this time, she began an Initiative to encourage interaction between all the Writing Groups along the North Coast of Northern Ireland, running regular workshops. She is also the Administer of a Facebook Page, open to all these Groups to distribute information and promote integrated activities between them.

Having created links with both Dr Frank Sewell and Dr Kathleen McCracken, Lecturers in Creative Writing at the Ulster University campus in Coleraine she regularly acts as an Auditor at their First and Third-year Creative Writing Workshops. With Reedsy Online Author Services , she is a member of the Judging Panel for their weekly Prompts Competitions.